VANCOUVER

The five sails of Canada Place glow in Vancouver's inner harbour

Vancouver is one of the world's most scenic, inviting, and livable cities. The Coast Mountain Range embraces the North Shore while the Pacific Ocean laps its accessible beaches, there is always a wealth of things for visitors and locals to do. Large enough to offer many diversions, small enough for visitors to soon feel at home, Vancouver offers its diversity to the world. This coastal city's physical beauty and attractions draw visitors from all over the world. Its West Coast Maritime Temperate climate promises warm summers and moderate winters.

Locals and visitors like nothing better than strolling in one of dozens of city parks and gardens. Some choose Stanley Park, noted for its 10.5-kilometre seawall perimeter. Others visit the VanDusen Botanical Gardens, or Queen Elizabeth Park, one of the oldest in the city. Still others enjoy the relaxed rhythms of Spanish Banks, with its vistas of mountains and ocean.

The lush green peninsula of 405-hectare (1000-acre) Stanley Park jutting into English Bay is a beloved landmark of the City of Vancouver. Within walking distance are downtown shopping malls and the boutiques of Robson Street. In the distance, the North Shore, with its village-like enclaves and soaring mountains, beckons visitors.

Twenty-four hours a day, 365 days a year, the Port of Vancouver hums with activity. Serving 90 countries, more than half the cargo handled here is destined for the Pacific Rim, including Japan, South Korea, and China. Built for the opening of Expo 86, the five Teflon-coated sails of Canada Place cover three city blocks.

More than 220 luxury cruise ships dock here every year, with passengers disembarking for sightseeing and shopping. Some 500,000 passengers visit annually enroute to Alaska.

Enjoy a stroll along the Canada Place Public Promenades or climb the Harbour Observation Deck for a fine view of Burrard Inlet. Canadian and international vessels share the waterway, while overhead light commuter planes come and go from destinations along the West Coast.

Home to the Vancouver Trade and Convention Centre and the Vancouver Board of Trade, Canada Place also houses a major hotel, restaurants, shops and art galleries. The CN IMAX Theatre, with its giant five-storey-high screen, seats 500 and runs year-round.

Rain or shine, the SeaBus, a double-ended catamaran, departs from nearby Waterfront Station for the 15-minute harbour ride to the North Shore's Lonsdale Quay. Built of lightweight aluminum, the SeaBus can turn, as well as stop, in its own length.

Opposite *Canada Place, built for Expo 86, juts into Burrard Inlet.*
Above *A cruise ship docks within minutes of downtown shopping centres.*

Robson Square is the centrepiece for two of Vancouver's architectural feats: The Vancouver Art Gallery, a former courthouse built in 1906, and the award-winning Vancouver Law Courts, opened in 1979. The chateau-style green roof of the Hotel Vancouver is a city landmark. Begun in 1929, the hotel took ten years to complete.

Above right *Colourful street flags flutter above Robson Street.*
Bottom right *In Vancouver, photo opportunities abound.*

Fireworks illuminate Vancouver's harbor in a dazzling display of colour. Year-round festivals are celebrated with spectacular fireworks displays over English Bay. Onlookers line West End beaches or watch from Kitsilano, on the south shore of the bay.

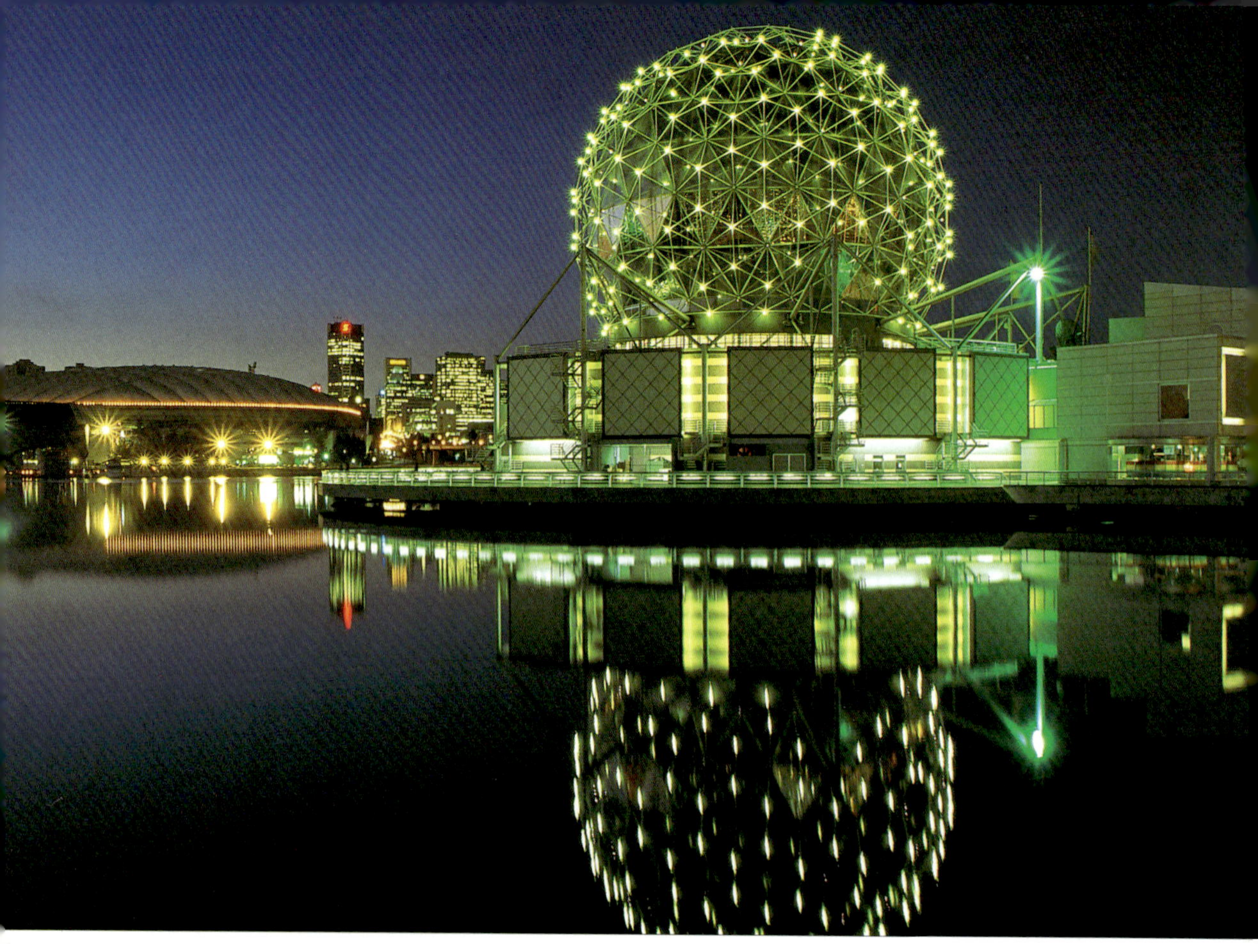

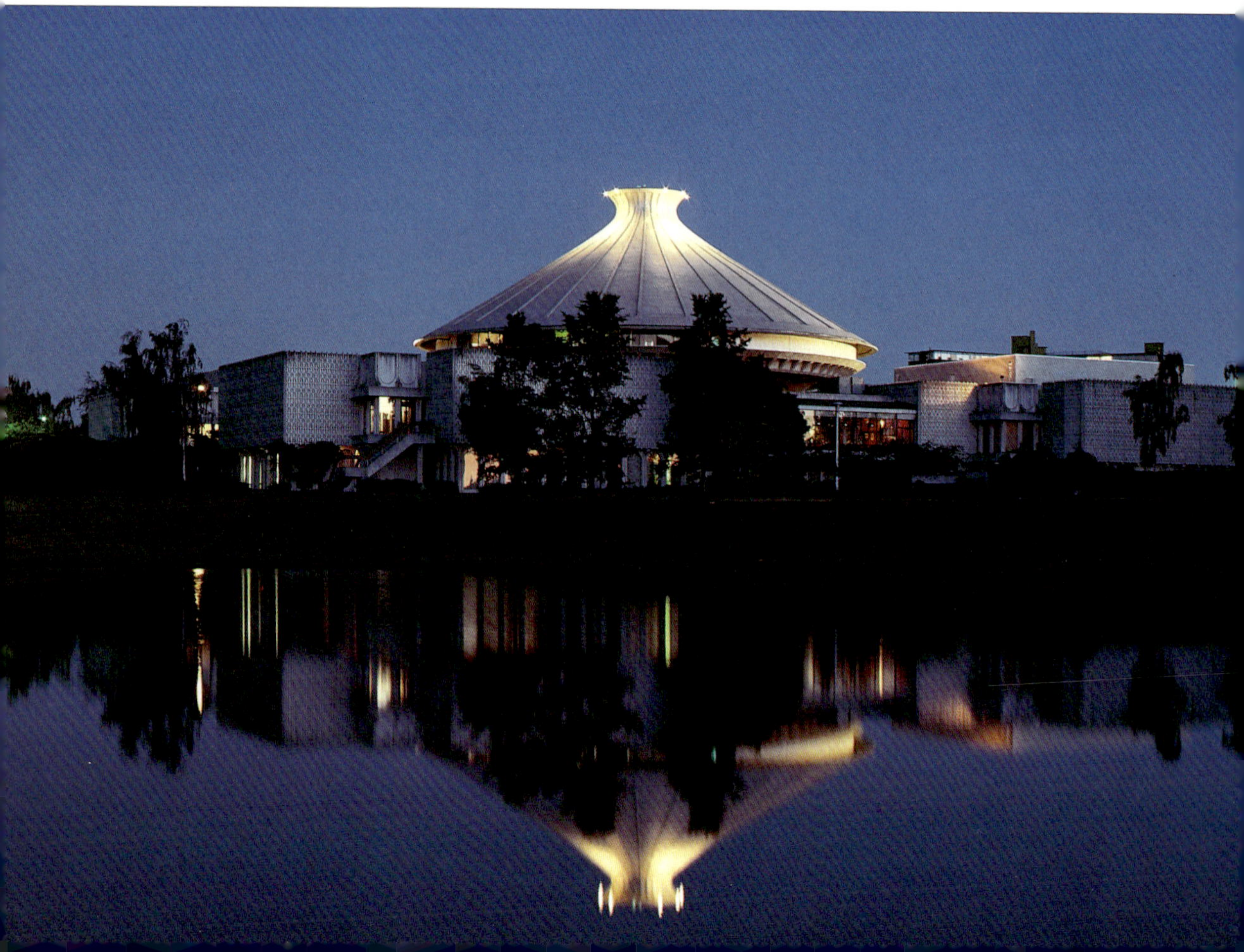

Located in the Lower Mainland, an area of 1.5 million residents, the city of Vancouver is the natural magnet for business, shopping and the arts. A variety of architectural textures and shapes characterize the downtown area, from the Teflon dome of BC Place Stadium to the light-studded geodesic dome of Science World. Just off Robson Square, the Vancouver Law Court is dominated by a dramatic sloping glass roof.

One of the most popular attractions, for residents and visitors alike, is Robson Street. Once known as Robsonstrasse for its Old World German restaurants and delicatessens, Robson and its environs are now international in scope. Leading fashion designers, including Chanel, Cartier, and Ferragamo, have opened shops here.

From Robson Street, it's a short walk to the Pacific Centre shopping mall, to the West End, English Bay and Stanley Park, or to False Creek.

High rises abound in the West End, resulting in one of the highest population densities in Canada. Yet the area does not feel overly crowded. As you stroll beyond Robson to Davie and Denman streets, bookstores, restaurants, cafés and souvenir shops roll past in delightful array.

Top opposite *The geodesic dome of Science World, reflected in False Creek.* **Bottom opposite** *Vanier Park's H.R. MacMillan Planetarium.* **Above** *The award-winning Vancouver Law Courts.*

Home to over 8000 species of aquatic life, the Vancouver Aquarium, located in Stanley Park, provides a look into the underwater habitats of the Pacific Northwest coast and elsewhere. The largest of Canada's aquariums and one of the largest in North America, it is visited by more than 800,000 people annually.

Whales, including friendly belugas and powerful killer whales, are the aquarium's major attraction. Housed in a new $10-million pool, killer whales—also known as orca—are presented in a naturalistic setting with guided whale watching sessions.

Four creative displays, the Amazon Forest, the Tropical Pacific Gallery, the Arctic Canada, and the Pacific Northwest displays, bring underwater environments to life.

Opposite *Beluga whales at feeding time.* **Above** *Bill Reid's sculpture,* Killer Whale, *at the Vancouver Aquarium.* **Below** *Aquarium visitors see nose to nose with residents.*

On September 27, 1889, Stanley Park was born. Named after Lord Stanley, then Governor General of Canada, it was dedicated "for the use and enjoyment of peoples of all colours, creeds and customes, for all time." Beloved by Vancouverites, the 405 hectares (1000 acres) of Stanley Park are located within minutes of downtown.

The outer rim of the park is circled by the 10.5-kilometre Stanley Park seawall, which connects its recreational areas: an aquarium, rowing and yacht clubs, playing fields, picnic areas, playgrounds, beaches, open air theatre, monuments and totem poles.

Visitors to Stanley Park may drive, walk or cycle around its perimeter, stopping to take in the sights at various locations.

Nesting along the seawall near the Warren Harding Memorial, great blue herons constantly arrive and depart throughout spring and early summer. Two of the herons' "vertical condominiums" are located directly east of the Harding Memorial.

The interior of the park, in contrast, is overgrown and wild. For the most part, it is densely forested, with a network of bike and foot paths. Beaver Lake, tucked in the centre, is a natural-state pond edged in cattails.

Opposite *Stanley Park features beaches and forest walks.* **Above** *Below Prospect Point, a cruise ship passes beneath the Lions Gate Bridge.*

Brockton Point's eight totem poles are a highlight of Stanley Park. The replicas represent North and South Kwakiutl, Haida, Nuu-chah-nulth and Nishga styles. Images on the poles include Thunderbird, with wings outstretched, and Raven, with extended beak.

On the sidewalks of Chinatown, vendors ply fruits and vegetables. Inside, rattan furniture, paper lanterns, silk blouses, and all manner of souvenirs are for sale. Chinese New Year parades wind past the Chinese Cultural Centre's Pavilion Gate.

Above *Chinatown's Pavilion Gate.*
Right *Chinese New Year's festivities feature lion and dragon dances.*

The year 1867 marked the arrival of Englishman Gassy Jack Deighton on the shore of Burrard Inlet. Within 24 hours, Deighton opened a saloon and Gastown was born. In its early years, Gastown was inhabited by hard-drinking, hard-living pioneers.

Gastown's most memorable landmark is located at the corner of Cambie and Water Streets. Based on an 1875 design, the Gastown steam clock is the only steam-operated clock in the world. On the hour, the Westminster chimes play merrily, while clouds of vapour from an underground system steam out the top.

Above *The gleam of Gastown by night, enhanced by heritage-style street lamps.*
Left *The steam clock chimes the hour.*

Once a False Creek industrial site, Granville Island was transformed in 1976. A spacious market, restaurants, live theatres, art school, marina, dozens of shops and a hotel have made the island a local favourite. In the Granville Island Market, fresh fruit and vegetables, baked goods, candies, cut flowers, gourmet coffees and quality crafts vie for attention. Children delight in the Kids Only Market and nearby water park.

> **Above** *A bird's eye view of Vancouver, looking toward the North Shore.* **Right** *A street band performs on Granville Island.* **Opposite top** *Granville Island services include a market, restaurants and craft galleries.* **Opposite bottom** *The Burrard Street Bridge was built in 1932.*

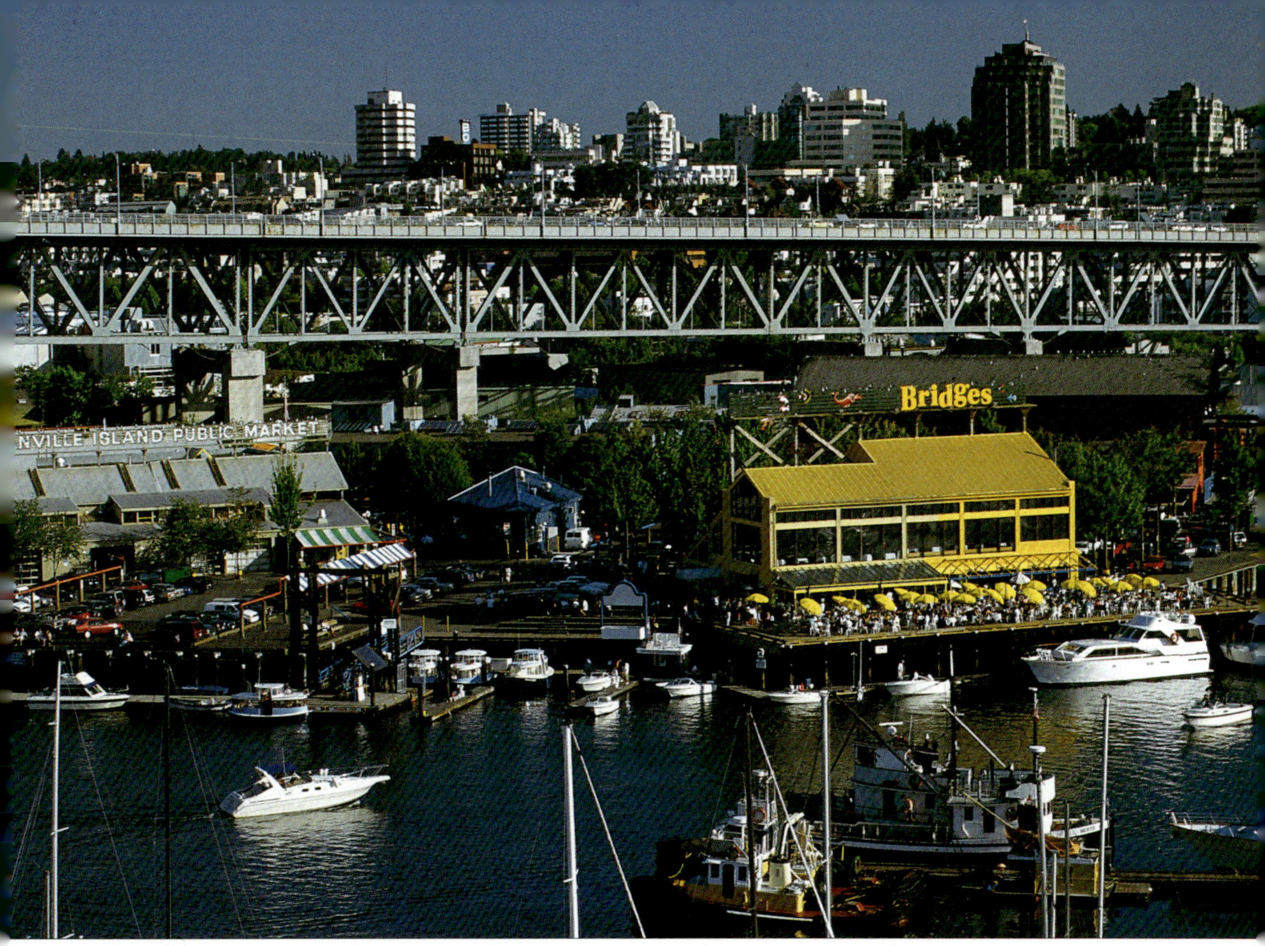
NVILLE ISLAND PUBLIC MARKET
Bridges

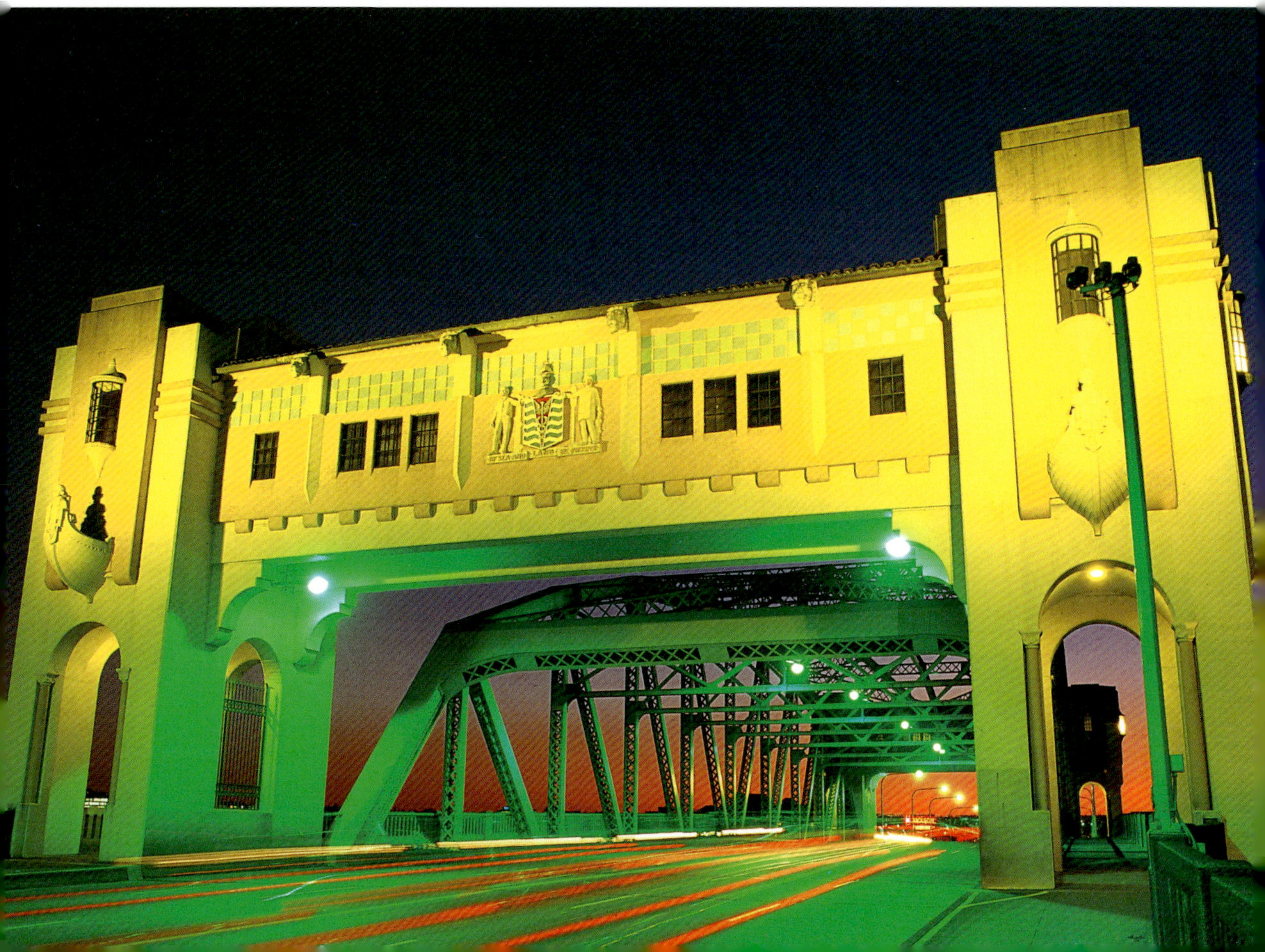

Famed for its aboriginal studies, the University of British Columbia (UBC) Museum of Anthropology sits on a bluff overlooking the Strait of Georgia. The museum's glass walls house an array of more than 12,000 Northwest Coast First Nations artifacts.

UBC is also noted for its public gardens. In addition to the UBC Botanical Garden, opened in 1916, visitors enjoy the BC Native Garden, the David C. Lam Asian Garden, and the Physick Garden, based on a 16th-century monastery herb garden.

There are more than three dozen parks and gardens accessible from downtown Vancouver. Stanley Park is one of the city's oldest, while the 800-hectare (2000-acre) Pacific Spirit Regional Park, near UBC, is one of the newest.

Distinctive public gardens display a variety of indigenous and introduced species. The VanDusen Botanical Gardens feature everything from a Rhododendron Walk to a Sino Himalayan Mountainscape, while Chinatown's Dr. Sun Yat-Sen Classical Chinese Garden is the only authentic classical garden constructed outside China.

Above *The Dr. Sun Yat-Sen Classical Chinese Garden.* **Opposite top** *A tranquil corner of the Nitobe Memorial Garden.* **Opposite bottom** *The Museum of Anthropology, inspired by a traditional Haida house.*

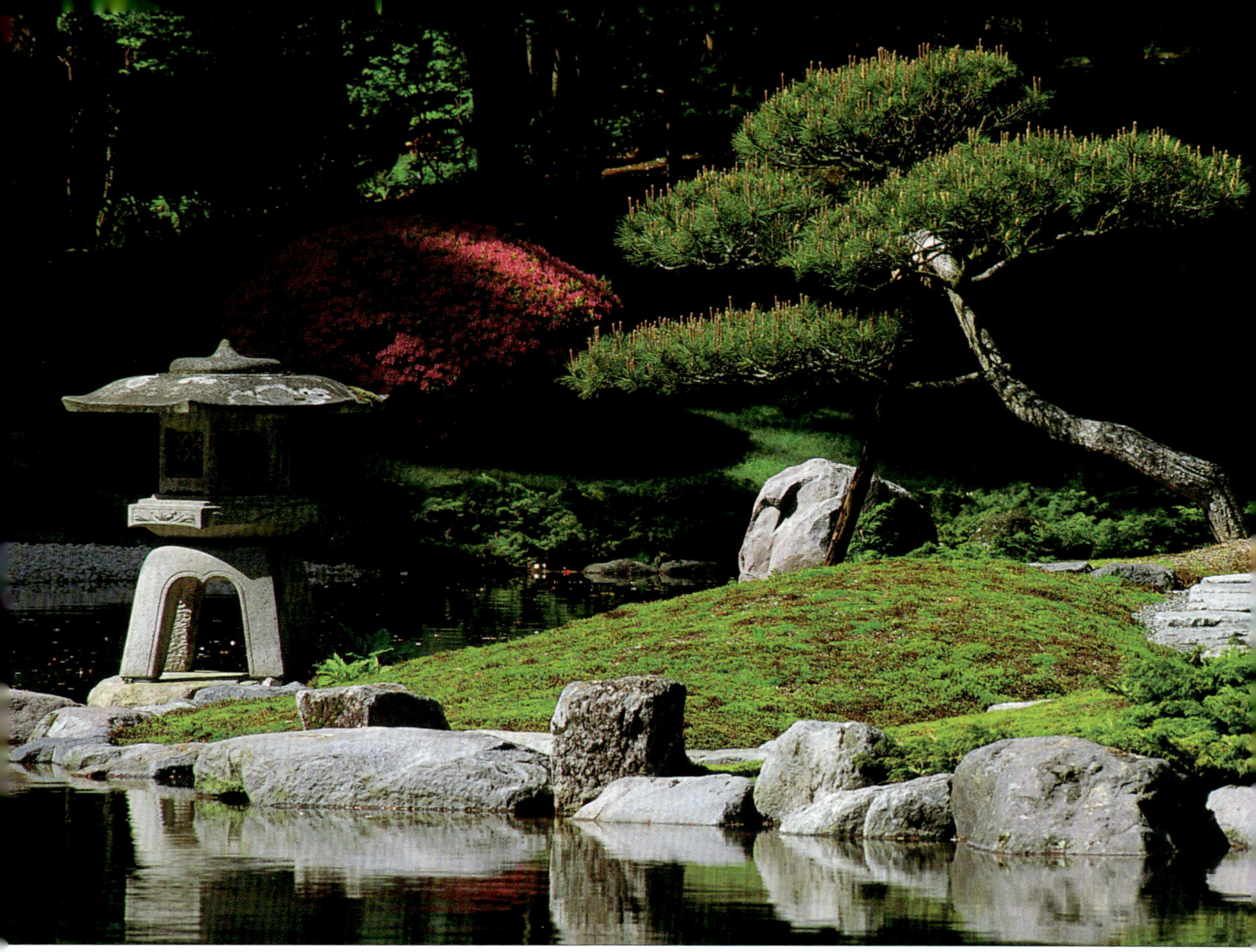

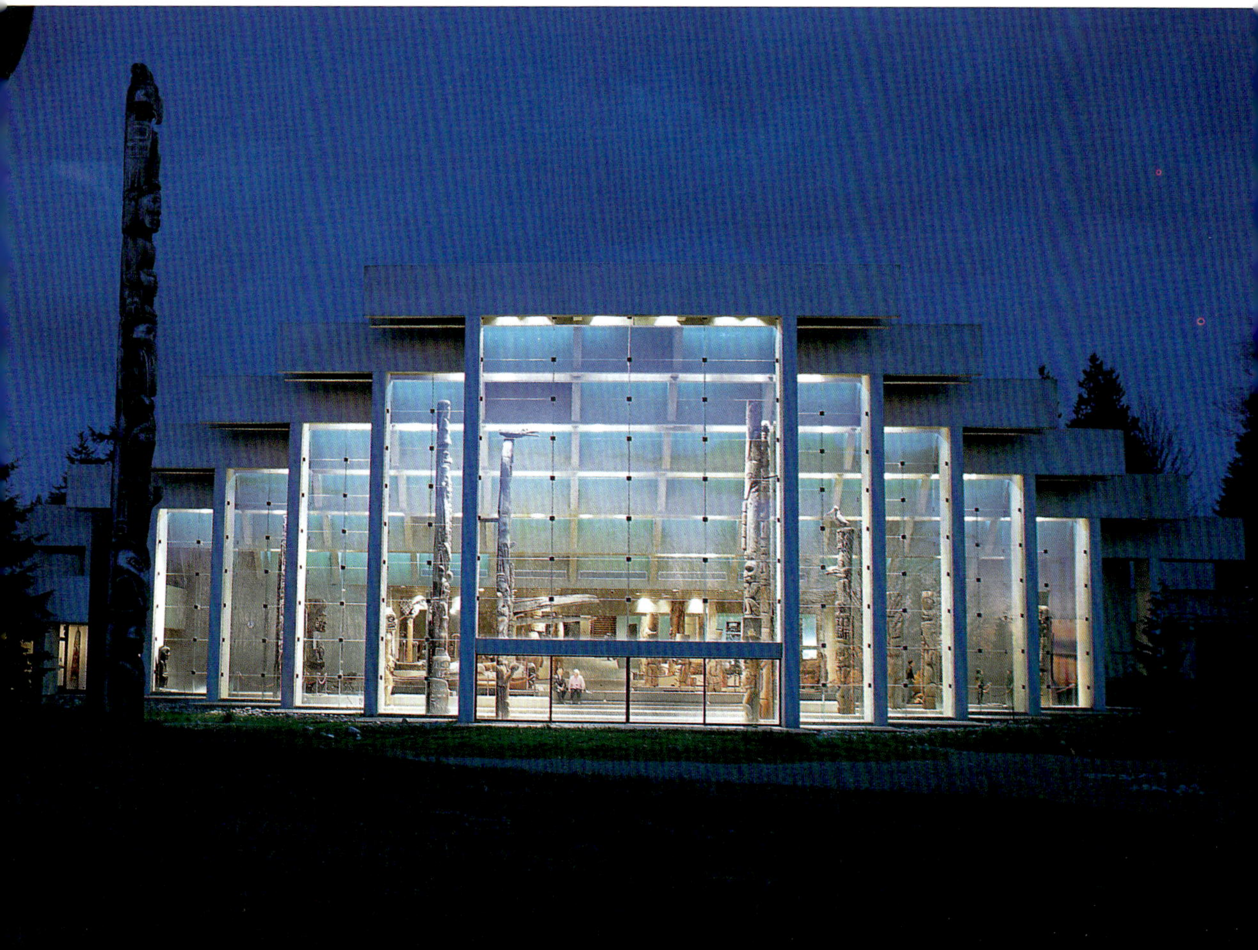

Opposite *Tulips bloom near Queen Elizabeth Park's Bloedel Floral Conservatory.* **Above top** *A quiet haven in one of the city's three dozen parks.* **Above bottom** *Springtime is gosling time in Stanley Park.*

On a sunny day, Vancouver beaches are crowded with well-oiled bodies lazing about. When the fall weather arrives, a quieter aspect presents itself. West Side beaches include Kitsilano, Jericho, Locarno, Spanish Banks and Wreak. The majority are family beaches; Wreak Beach, however, is the city's unofficial nudist beach. In the West End Stanley Park's Second Beach is popular for its salt water swimming pool, playground, baseball diamonds and picnic areas.

Above *From Vanier Park, it's a short sail across English Bay to the West End.* **Right** *The Vancouver Children's Festival is an annual event.* **Opposite top** *Sunset over the Strait of Georgia.* **Opposite bottom** *A leisurely autumn walk on a Vancouver beach.*

When first built, the 450-metre-long Lions Gate Bridge was one of the longest suspension bridges in the world. The garlanded structure lights the way to West and North Vancouver, Grouse Mountain, Mount Seymour, and up Howe Sound to Whistler and Blackcomb Mountains.

The North Shore is a blend of nature, posh residential neighbourhoods, village-like enclaves, and modern shopping centres. Both Ambleside and Dundarave in West Vancouver retain the flavour of traditional seaside villages; North Vancouver's cosy Deep Cove, to the east, is tucked away on Indian Arm.

Lonsdale Quay in North Vancouver is a major retail centre, complete with public market, hotel and entertainment complex.

Opposite *The Capilano Suspension Bridge swings 70 metres above the canyon floor.* **Inset** *A friendly welcome.* **Top** *A view of the Lions Gate Bridge.* **Bottom** *The SeaBus crosses to the North Shore in 15 minutes.*

Marine Drive snakes along Howe Sound to the inviting West Vancouver village of Horseshoe Bay. The village was once known to its Native inhabitants as Chai-hai, meaning a low sizzling noise—probably made by small fish jumping along the shore. Today a more likely sound is the hoot of a BC Ferry enroute to Vancouver Island, the Sunshine Coast, or Bowen Island.

For a unique journey north, board the Royal Hudson Steam Train, the last steam locomotive still in service in Canada. The Royal Hudson has travelled the North Vancouver-Squamish route more than 2000 times. Return, if you like, aboard the M.V. Britannia Passenger Ferry.

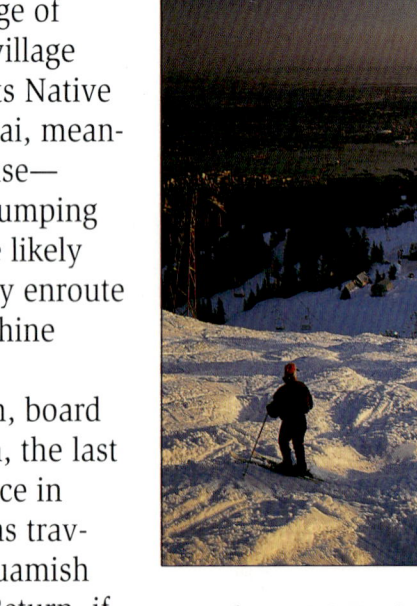

Above BC Ferries leave Horseshoe Bay daily for coastal destinations.
Bottom Skiing on Grouse Mountain, with Vancouver in the distance.